Chapl
of Mary

Our Lady of Kibeho
Mother of the Word

Catholic Diocese of Gikongoro
Kibeho Edition © 2021
Rwanda

ISBN 978 1 7399 299 1 6

Cover picture:
Original wooden sculpture of Our Lady of Kibeho, Mother of the
Word, Sanctuary of Our Lady of Sorrows of Kibeho, Kibeho,
Rwanda

CONTENTS

INTRODUCTION

Our Lady of Kibeho, Mother of the Word, appeared in Kibeho from the 28th November 1981 to the 28th of November 1989 to:

1) Alphonsine Mumureke
2) Nathalie Mukamazimpaka
3) Marie Claire Mukangango

Only these visionaries have been officially recognized and approved by the Catholic Church in 2001.

Our Lady of Kibeho's main messages are:

"Repent, Pray and Convert your hearts."

"If you pray the Chaplet of the Seven Sorrows meditatively, you will get the strength you need to repent."

"I want all Christians to meditate on the Seven Sorrows Chaplet and pray for the world which is becoming very rebellious."

Our Lady invites us to pray without hypocrisy, to have more faith, to follow the Gospel, to pray for all families, for the Church, for all nations and political leaders so that we can persevere on the path of conversion of the heart and enjoy justice and peace.

This prayer book contains especially the Chaplet of the Seven Sorrows which Our Lady of Kibeho, Mother of the Word, invites us to pray for the whole world.

I thank all people who will pray and meditate on the Gospel, and spread the messages of The Mother of the Word, imitating her virtues of humility, patience, and deep faith in God.
She will continue to help us in all spheres of our lives, as She intercedes and prays for us.

Célestin HAKIZIMANA
Bishop of Gikongoro
Imprimatur
28th of December 2020

Do we know how to pray?

Our Lady of Kibeho, said to Nathalie Mukamazimpaka:
"The one who prays should be engaged, present, with humility from the heart, knowing what is being asked and its implications. Above all, one should have total confidence in God and be patient."

Nathalie asked: *"Every time you tell us to pray always with all our hearts and minds, does it mean that we do not know how to pray and that we never do it well?"*

Our Lady replied: *"It is only in words that you know it, but when you want to practise what you say you know, something else happens. There are many who try to do it well, but their hearts are often elsewhere, and they are taken up by so many other things. That is why I have come: to remind you, to shake the conscience of the absent-minded ones, and to recollect those who have been taken up by worldly concerns; so that you may fulfill your duty to pray without disturbances and distractions."*

Our Lady of Kibeho has given us a few suggestions on how to improve the quality of our prayers. She said:
"I want all Christians to meditate on the Seven Sorrows Chaplet and pray for the world which is becoming very rebellious."

"If you recite the Chaplet of the Seven Sorrows meditatively, you will get the strength you need to repent."

"You need to maintain the force of prayer without hypocrisy and to persevere on the path of conversion of the heart."

"Let nothing keep you away from prayer."

"My children, pray, pray, follow the Gospel of my Son and put it in practice; doing so will surely benefit your soul!"

In Lk 11:1, one of the disciples asked Jesus: *"Lord, teach us to pray ..."* and Jesus taught the Words of the "Our Father." This is why it is called The Lord's Prayer. The fuller version is in Mt 6:9-13.

Jesus performed many signs and miracles before He taught this Prayer. The desire to pray was born in the heart of the disciples by being with Him and seeing the way He prayed. Having seen Him pray, they wanted to pray like Him. The disciples learnt the "Our Father" directly from Jesus, and we can also deduce that Our Lady prayed the "Our Father" as well.

When we pray The Lord's Prayer, we bless God Our
Father, and when we pray The Hail Mary, we bless both
Jesus and His Mother Mary. That is what we do when
we pray the Rosary and the Chaplet, in addition to
meditating and contemplating on the life of Jesus and
Mary.

At the end of Lk 11:13 Jesus said that the Heavenly
Father will give the Holy Spirit to those who ask Him.
Therefore, we need to pray asking for the Holy Spirit. A
simple invocation: *"Holy Spirit, help me!"* was
suggested by Alphonsine Mumureke who also reminds
us that *"Prayer is a dialogue with The Lord ... We need
to talk less about God and talk to God instead. It is
more important to talk to the Virgin Mary rather than
talk about Her. If I don't cultivate this dialogue/prayer
between myself and the Virgin Mary, what can I say?
That I am using my intelligence, but not my heart."*
*"What quality time have I given the Word of God in my
life? How much time have I given to the Word of God?"*

We need to read the Holy Scriptures, The Word of God.
We need to read it slowly and meditatively and God will
speak to us when we pray.

Prayer needs to go beyond our individual needs.

Our Lady tells us that we have a "duty to pray" and She
asks us to pray always and wholeheartedly, and to pray

intensely for the world. We are asked to offer prayers of intercession. Jesus intercedes for us, Our Lady intercedes for us, and we also are called to pray and intercede for the world.

A simple act of contrition (a prayer in itself) is that of the blind man in the Gospel who begged Jesus saying: *"Son of David, have Mercy on me!"* Mk 11:47b.

The blind man regained his sight because he believed that Jesus could heal him.

In Mt 9:22, the woman said to herself that if she could only touch the cloak of Jesus she would be healed, and she was. Jesus said to her:

"Courage, your faith has saved you."

At the heart of each Hail Mary is the Holy Name of Jesus, who said: *"Whatever you ask in my name, I will do it, that the Father may be glorified in the Son; if you ask anything in my name, I will do it."* Jn 14:13-14

Our Lady is a model of prayer and faith. Prayer and faith go together, you cannot have one without the other. We need to pray and ask for a deeper faith.

But is there enough faith? Will there be enough faith? (Lk 18:8) Our Lady wants us to have more faith, and that is the main reason for Marian apparitions.

Our Lady of Kibeho said: *"In all your family problems, do put yourself under the Holy Family's patronage."*

Jesus said: *"Take my yoke upon you and learn from me, for I am gentle and humble of heart, and you will find rest."* Mt 11:28-29

Prayer is time to rest and listen to God.

What would our lives be if they were not interspersed with prayer? We need to balance the demands of our lives and make time to read the Gospel and pray. In prayer we find rest.

During a talk to a group of pilgrims in Kibeho, Nathalie said: *"We should pray with simplicity and humility. We need to let go of bad habits and detach ourselves from what hinders us from getting closer to God.*

Those who pray mechanically and only for themselves pray badly. Instead, we need to pray slowly and meditatively and we need to pray for other people and for the Catholic Church which is being persecuted.

We need to pray for those who suffer, including the Souls in Purgatory. We also need to pray for those who cause suffering so that they may change and convert to God. This would make it possible for the world to have peace."

Prayers need to be accompanied by participation in the Sacrament of Reconciliation and the Sacrament of the Holy Eucharist.

The historical background of the Chaplet is linked to seven noblemen in Florence, Italy. They used to express their devotion to Our Lady by singing lauds in front of her image painted on the wall in the street. On the 15th of August 1233, the feast of the Assumption of Our Lady, the image came alive and Our Lady of Sorrows appeared to them dressed in black, because of the hate and killing that divided Florence at the time. The young men put on black clothes and went up to Mount Senario to lead a life of prayer and penance. The Order of the Servites, the Servants of Mary, was later established with a special devotion to Mary, Mother of Sorrows. From then on, the Seven Sorrows Chaplet began to spread around the world, including Rwanda.

Sister Thérèse Kamugisha, the mother superior of the Benebikira nuns (daughters of Mary) saw the Blessed Virgin Mary in a dream. Our Lady, holding the Seven Sorrows rosary, said to her: *"Please, teach my children!"* When she was mother superior between 1953 and 1964 she did just that. But after her death the devotion and practice was neglected and forgotten.

On the 3rd of March 1982, Our Lady of Kibeho asked Marie Claire if she knew the Seven Sorrows Chaplet. She didn't and she was given the task to find out. The elderly nuns remembered little, so Our Lady took it upon herself to teach Marie Claire.

When Marie Claire Mukangango asked why the Seven Sorrows Chaplet had sunk into oblivion, Our Lady replied that people generally seek what gives them pleasure, and instinctively avoid everything that is painful. This Chaplet reminds us of the way of the Sorrowful Mysteries that Jesus and Mary endured to save people's souls. Suffering is a reality in this life.

The most important elements of the Chaplet are the act of contrition and the meditations on the Sorrows.

Marie Claire Mukangango was asked to dip her fingers in holy water, make the sign of the Holy Cross and reflect on her morality every day (examination of conscience and act of contrition).

Our Lady showed her how to pray the Chaplet of the Seven Sorrows. Our Lady also told her to pray it at least on Tuesdays and Fridays. Marie Claire was encouraged to share her contemplation and meditation aloud, so that other people could learn to meditate themselves. She was also told to inform the headmistress, the parish priest and the Bishop so that the Chaplet could be prayed regularly by the whole Church, because Our Lady said She came not only for Kibeho, but for the whole world.

Marie Claire experienced a vivid vision of the Passion of Christ, and, moved by compassion, wept as she meditated and shared the suffering of Jesus and Mary.

The Chaplet begins with an act of contrition.

By meditating on the suffering of the Blessed Virgin Mary we unite with the Passion of Christ and offer our sufferings which are purified and transformed into prayer.

By meditating on the suffering of the Blessed Virgin Mary and Jesus as they escaped to Egypt, we can also remember the sufferings of families, war refugees, migrants, the homeless and the persecuted. By doing so, we can pray for them, and offer practical assistance, remembering that the Passion of Christ is followed by the joy and the glory of the Resurrection. Our Christian calling is ultimately to share in that joy, even when suffering. We put our faith into practice by performing acts of charity, a concrete way of expressing our love towards God and our brothers and sisters.

When Marie Claire asked Our Lady why She came to Kibeho, Our Lady replied that in Kibeho there were still humble people who loved her and were not attached to wealth and money.

On the 15th of August 1982, the feast of the Assumption, Our Lady appeared in tears (as in

Florence). Marie Claire was asked what she was doing to make the Seven Sorrows Chaplet known (We ought to ask ourselves the same question!).

Marie Claire's apparitions ended on the 15th of September, the memorial of Our Lady of Sorrows.

Meditation on the second Sorrow of the Chaplet

by Sister Alphonsine Mumureke. Extracts from:
"Our Lady of Kibeho, Mother of the Word" Published by the Diocese of Gikongoro, ISBN 978 1 7399299 0 9

"Why escape to Egypt? Because Herod threatened to kill Jesus. I can meditate on all the cases that provoke an escape: for example a separated couple where a woman is forced to flee from the family, the people who are forced to flee because there is something to fear and their life is in danger. We too are occasionally threatened by awful things.

For me there is also another escape, the spiritual one. For example, you hide yourself to pray. Going to Church to pray is a kind of escape from the world, to pray, to seek a moment of recollection, to listen to what the Lord tells us.

These groups that meet to listen to the Word of God, to give each other advice, is a little escape for the good of their soul. We need the spiritual flight to be able to speak to God.

There are people who say: *"For two days I want to pray, I will not answer calls, I will not open the internet. I will not see the television."* This is a Spiritual flight. *"Today is for the Lord, I put everything aside."* Everything I do, every moment, let it be for the glory of God, for the Church, for the Pope.

Yes, we are believers and the Church is our Mother, as your mother is part of your life, the Church is part of our life. The Holy Mass is the time to pray for the Church, for the Pope, for the priests who have the task of bringing the living Jesus into people's hearts, into our hearts.

We need to pray for the Church and the family.

The Virgin Mary is the Mother of the Church. She does not come for Her Sorrows. She comes for Her Son, it is Her participation in our salvation. She participated in the Passion of Christ, She comes for Christ, not for Herself. What She experienced as Sorrow is in the name of Her Son, for the salvation of humanity. She is therefore the collaborator, being the Mother.

The Chaplet of the Seven Sorrows begins with the Sign of the Cross. The Sign of the Cross is important, it drives away evil spirits. The evil one is afraid of the Cross.

As soon as you wake up, before putting your feet on the floor, you start with the sign of the Cross. The Cross is important. It is the sign of our salvation. And Jesus had to go through it in order to send us the Holy Spirit.

It is better to say "Chaplet" of the Seven Sorrows of Mary, so that people will not confuse it with the "Rosary" of the Sorrowful Mysteries of Jesus.

The Virgin Mary, despite being the Mother of God, has participated in this suffering of Her Son Jesus.

Jesus had the capacity to suffer alone, without including His Mother.

Sometimes a person is afraid to confront suffering, nonetheless it is part of us.

There are people who suffer and they don't recognise God, they spend money to alleviate a suffering that will never end. These people need our prayers.

From the moment Jesus came into our lives, the suffering we have, we carry it with joy, knowing that God has carried it with us. Therefore, I have to accept the crosses that come my way in this life, because you cannot say that you are called only to joy. I have to go through what Jesus went through. And Jesus came to purify suffering.

His Most Holy Mother has collaborated with the "Salvific plan" of her Son to show us that we have known Christ. There is no way to contemplate the

Father if we do not dare go through this way of suffering.

I suffer also for what I see outside, in the world, but in faith, without despairing. This is where joy is born. It is because I know that all these things I see, the sufferings, these awful things, God has taken it upon Himself. The Virgin Mary comes to help us meditate on this.

In Kibeho, the Virgin Mary talked a lot about suffering. Now I realise why. But also outside Rwanda there are many awful things that don't shed blood. For these things, if I don't live with God who gave His life for us, I could end up in despair.

If I were to ask: *"Lord, where are we going with these things, do you really exist?"*

He would reply: *"Yes, I exist because I have carried all this on the Cross with me. Don't be afraid."*

Looking at Christ Crucified, I am not afraid of these things that I see in the world, these very awful things.

If I don't want to meditate on the episode of old Simeon who announces to the Virgin Mary the suffering of Her Son, who amongst us, in this life has not ever received awful news? Because to meditate on this will help me to live with a suffering that I cannot explain. Because it exists. There is no reason for suffering, but it exists. There is no reason for evil, but it exists. This is why I have to pray to the Lord who has lived with me, so that in His suffering, I may draw the strength to overcome what I am going through.

The message of suffering is a really important message in a Christian family. And we cannot caress a person who does not want to accept suffering, because suffering is not a malediction, it has to be accepted. There is suffering and we need to accept it.

Joy and suffering are part of our life.

What gives me joy is Christ resurrected for me. This is our joy. Joy is born meditating on the Seven Sorrows of Mary, because we have God, who has gone through these sufferings to save us. Ah, what I am living is not dramatic, it is a normal thing! Tuesdays and Fridays, this is really my prayer throughout the day."

For more information:
friendsofthemotheroftheword@gmail.com
Friends of The Mother of The Word

Chaplet of the Seven Sorrows of Mary

With Mary, we contemplate and meditate on the Passion of Christ.

Sign of the Cross: In the name of the Father, and of the Son, and of the Holy Spirit. Amen.

Prayer to the Holy Spirit (prayer of your choice)

Opening Prayer: My God, I offer you this Chaplet of Sorrows for your Most Holy Glory and to honour your Most Holy Mother. I will meditate and share her Sorrows. I beg you to grant me contrition for the sins that I have committed. Grant me the grace to be meek and humble, that I may receive the indulgences offered in this Chaplet.

Act of Contrition: (moment of silence)

"To me, a sinner, and to all sinners, grant perfect contrition for our sins!"(x3)

*After each Sorrow: *Reading and Meditation on the Gospel, *Our Father; 7 Hail Marys; **"Mother of Mercy, remind us each day of the Passion of Christ."*

First Sorrow: Mary listens and accepts in faith the Prophecy of St. Simeon. Lk 2:25-35

Second Sorrow: Mary escapes to Egypt with Jesus and Joseph. Mt 2:13-15

Third Sorrow: Mary goes in search of Jesus in Jerusalem. Lk 2:41-52

Fourth Sorrow: Mary meets Jesus on the way to Calvary. Lk 23:26-29

Fifth Sorrow: Mary stands beneath the Cross of Jesus, Crucified for our Redemption. Jn 19:25-34

Sixth Sorrow: Mary receives the body of Jesus. Jn 19:38-40

Seventh Sorrow: Mary lays the body of Jesus in the tomb, awaiting the Resurrection. Jn 19:41-42

Closing Prayer: Mary, Queen of Martyrs, your soul has endured deep sorrow. I beg you, for the tears you shed in these mysterious moments, to obtain for me, and for all sinners, a sincere repentance. Amen.

Invocation: Heart of Most Holy Mary, who suffered immensely despite being Immaculate, pray for us who take refuge in you. *(Repeat Invocation x3)*

Novena in honour of Our Lady of Kibeho[1]

Main theme: *"Produce good fruits as evidence of your repentance." (Lk 3:8a)*

Day 1: Sign of the Cross, Marian Song - your choice
Meditation on the Word of God: Mk 1:14-15
Message of Our Lady: *"Repent! Repent! Repent!"*
"Convert your heart while there is still time." "Convert yourself without delay and return to the Lord."
Prayer and Meditation on the Chaplet of the Seven Sorrows
Marian song
Prayer to Our Lady of Kibeho

Day 2: Sign of the Cross, Marian Song
Meditation on the Word of God: Mt 24:4-13
Message of Our Lady: *"Pray constantly for the conversion of the world." "The world is rebellious against God, it commits too many sins, it has neither love nor peace." "If you do not repent and do not convert your hearts, you will fall into the abyss."*
 Prayer and Meditation on the Chaplet
 Marian Song
 Prayer to Our Lady of Kibeho

---

[1] The Feast of Our Lady of Kibeho is on the 28th of November. The Novena starts on the 19th of November till the 27th.

20

Day 3: **Sign of the Cross, Marian Song**
Meditation on the Word of God: 2 P 2:1-3
Message: *"Faith and unbelief will come together in a way hard to distinguish."*
The Virgin Mary suffers to see that people do not want to repent. The visionaries said to have seen the Virgin Mary crying on August the 15th, 1982. The Mother of God was very sad because of people's unbelief and lack of repentance. She complained of our way of life, characterised by low moral standards, evil inclination, and continuous disobedience of God's Commandments.
Prayer and Meditation on the Chaplet
Marian Song
Prayer to Our Lady of Kibeho

Day 4: Sign of the Cross, Marian Song
Meditation on the Word of God: Sir 2:1-6
Message: *"No one will reach heaven without having suffered." "A child of Mary does not reject suffering."*
(The Blessed Virgin Mary to Nathalie). For Christians, "unavoidable suffering" is a means of compensating for the sins of the world and participating in the suffering of Jesus and Mary for the salvation of the world.
Prayer and Meditation on the Chaplet
Marian Song
Prayer to Our Lady of Kibeho

Day 5: Sign of the Cross, Marian Song
Meditation on the Word of God: Ep 6:18
Message: *"Pray always and wholeheartedly."*
People are not praying, and those who do pray, do not
pray with a sincere heart.
The Blessed Virgin Mary asks us to pray frequently and
sincerely for the whole world, to teach others to pray
and to pray for those who do not pray. She asks us to
pray with greater zeal and purity of heart.
Prayer and Meditation on the Chaplet
Marian Song
Prayer to Our Lady of Kibeho

Day 6: Sign of the Cross, Marian Song
Meditation on the Word of God: Mt 6: 5-8
Message: *"Pray and meditate regularly on the Chaplet*
of the Seven Sorrows of Mary."
The Mother of the Word told Marie Claire to make the
Seven Sorrows Chaplet known throughout the Church.
The purpose of this Chaplet is to help us meditate on the
Passion of Jesus and the great Sorrows of His Mother.
When it is recited well, it has the power to renew and
convert our hearts, it gives us the strength to fear sin and
run away from it because it is sin that puts Christ Jesus
on the Cross. Someone who meditates on it properly
finds the power to perform the acts which testify to

one's inner conversion: a thirst for meditating every day on the mysteries of the Cross of Jesus, the Saviour of people, to unite with Him in his suffering, and those of His Mother. This Chaplet is recited especially on Tuesdays and Fridays.

Prayer and Meditation on the Chaplet
Marian Song
Prayer to Our Lady of Kibeho

Day 7: Sign of the Cross, Marian Song
Meditation on the Word of God: Jn 2:1-5
Message: *Marian Devotions* - expressed through sincere and regular prayer of the Chaplet and Rosary.
Prayer and Meditation on the Chaplet
Marian Song
Prayer to Our Lady of Kibeho

Day 8: Sign of the Cross, Marian Song
Meditation on the Word of God: 1 Th 5:12-22
Message: *"Pray always for the Church, many troubles will be upon it in times to come."* (The Blessed Virgin Mary to Alphonsine Mumureke).
Prayer and Meditation on the Chaplet
Marian Song
Prayer to Our Lady of Kibeho

Day 9: Sign of the Cross, Marian Song
Meditation on the Word of God: Rv 21:1-4
Message: Our Lady requested the building of a Chapel in Kibeho (16th of January & 4th of September 1982). Let's pray and praise the Virgin Mary!
Kibeho is a meeting place for the seekers of God, who come to pray and learn at the school of the Virgin Mary, a high place of conversion, of reparations for the sins of the world, and reconciliation; a rallying point for those who were scattered as well as for those who love the values of compassion and fraternity without borders, a high place reminiscent of the Gospel of the Cross of Christ.
Prayer and Meditation on the Chaplet
Marian Song
Prayer to Our Lady of Kibeho
Closing Prayer: *The Magnificat:* (Lk 1:46-55)

Gikongoro, 8th of December 2017
Imprimatur
Célestin HAKIZIMANA
Bishop of GIKONGORO Diocese

Prayer to Our Lady of Kibeho

(+Bishop Augustin Misago, 1st of October 2007)

Lord our God, we thank you for the good things which you always give us and your infinite goodness in sending us the Blessed Virgin Mary, Mother of the Word, so that She may come to bring us back to the good path that Jesus Christ your Son showed us.

She asked us to repent, to confess our sins and to pray without hypocrisy. However we have disobeyed, hardened our hearts and this has been the source of our misfortune.

Thus, Lord our God, we beseech you through Jesus Christ your Son, to have mercy on us and to forgive us.

Lord, have Mercy on us! (x 3 tapping your chest.)

And you, Our Mother, Virgin Mother of the Word, we thank you for having accomplished the mission of God, for your patience towards us, suffering by shedding lots of tears when you saw that we refused to receive the message that you brought. But, from this moment on, we commit ourselves to be faithful children by doing all that the Lord tells us, by following the advice that you gave us here at Kibeho, and by fortifying the love to transform ourselves into beautiful flowers whose scent is pleasant everywhere for everyone.

Virgin Mary, Mother of the Word, pray for us. Amen.

Come Holy Spirit

Come Holy Spirit, fill the hearts of your faithful,
enkindle in us the fire of Your Love.
Heavenly King, Consoler Spirit, Spirit of Truth, present
everywhere, fill all things;
treasure of all good and source of all life,
come dwell in us, cleanse and save us,
You who are all Good! Amen.

Act of Contrition

O my God, I repent with all my heart for all my sins
because I have offended you who are infinitely good and
worthy of love.
With the help of your Grace I sincerely resolve never to
offend you again and to avoid situations that would lead
me to sin. Amen.

Act of entrustment to the Holy Family

O Holy Family of Nazareth, Jesus, Mary and Joseph, to
You we entrust our families. Amen.

The Magnificat: Mary's Song of praise

My soul magnifies the Lord, and my spirit rejoices in God my Saviour, for He has looked at the humility of His handmaid.

From now on all generations will call me blessed, for The Almighty has done great things in me, and Holy is His name.

From generation to generation His mercy is on those who fear him.

He has shown the power of His arm, He has scattered the proud-hearted.

He has overthrown the powerful from their thrones and has lifted up the humble.

He has filled the hungry with good things; He has sent the rich away empty.

He has come to the help of Israel, His servant, remembering His mercy, according to the promise made to our fathers, to Abraham and to his descendants, forever.

Lk 1:46-55